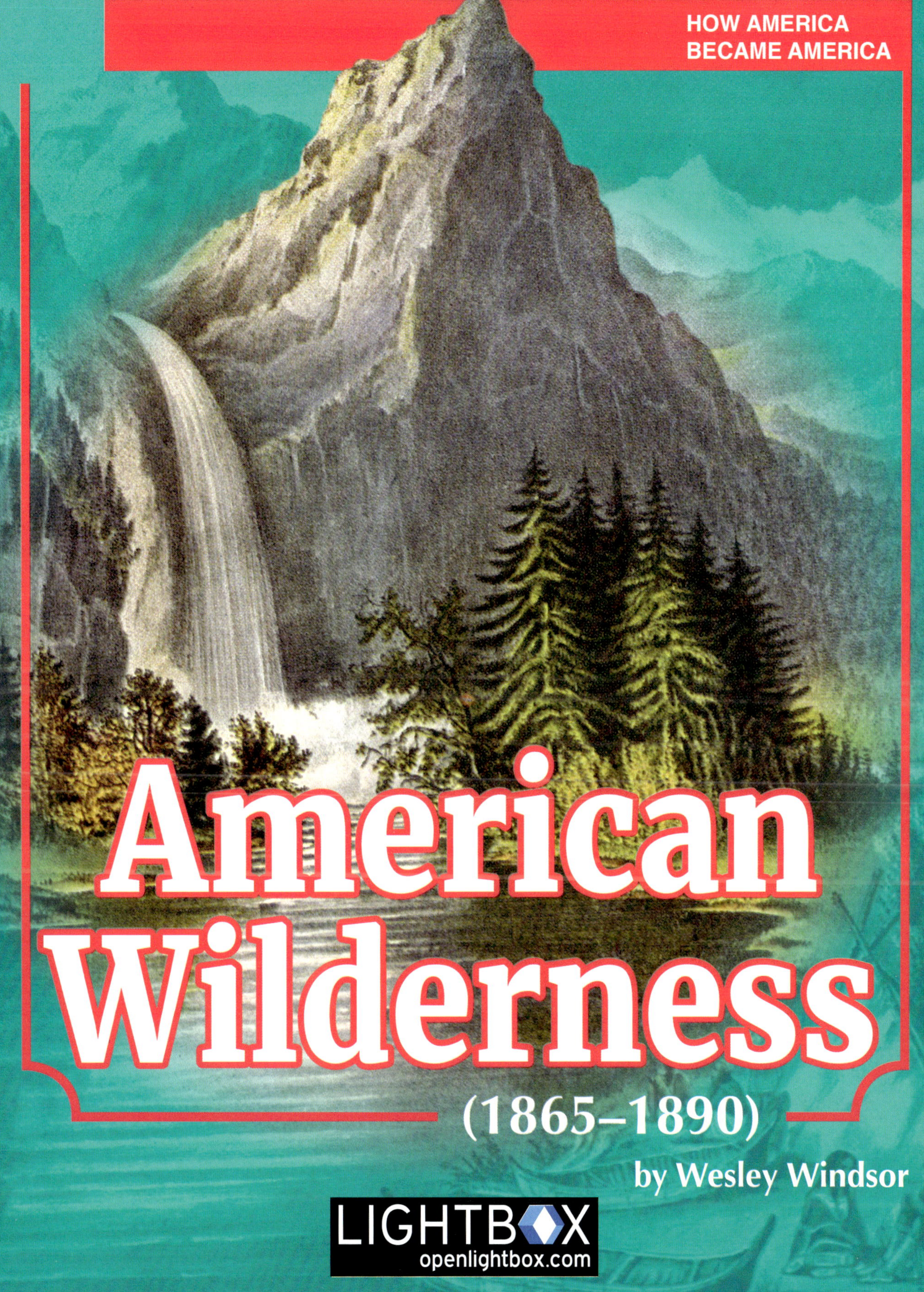
HOW AMERICA
BECAME AMERICA
American
Wilderness
(1865–1890)
by Wesley Windsor
LIGHTBOX
openlightbox.com

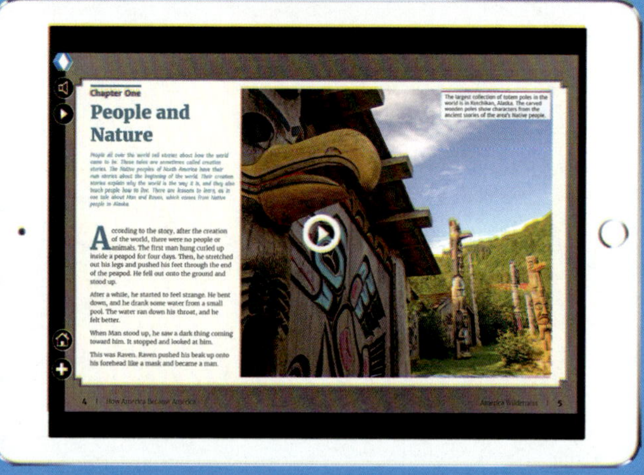

Lightbox is an all-inclusive digital solution for the teaching and learning of curriculum topics in an original, groundbreaking way. Lightbox is based on National Curriculum Standards.

STANDARD FEATURES OF LIGHTBOX

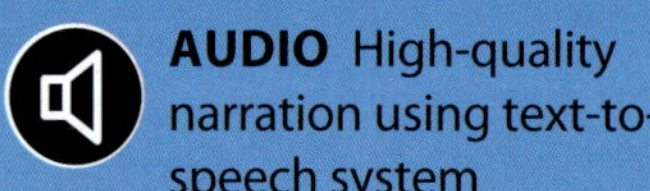
AUDIO High-quality narration using text-to-speech system

ACTIVITIES Printable PDFs that can be emailed and graded

SLIDESHOWS Pictorial overviews of key concepts

VIDEOS Embedded high-definition video clips

WEBLINKS Curated links to external, child-safe resources

TRANSPARENCIES Step-by-step layering of maps, diagrams, charts, and timelines

INTERACTIVE MAPS Interactive maps and aerial satellite imagery

QUIZZES Ten multiple choice questions that are automatically graded and emailed for teacher assessment

KEY WORDS Matching key concepts to their definitions

Contents

Chapter One

People and Nature

People all over the world tell stories about how the world came to be. These tales are sometimes called creation stories. The Native peoples of North America have their own stories about the beginning of the world. Their creation stories explain why the world is the way it is, and they also teach people how to live. There are lessons to learn, as in one tale about Man and Raven, which comes from Native people in Alaska.

According to the story, after the creation of the world, there were no people or animals. The first man hung curled up inside a peapod for four days. Then, he stretched out his legs and pushed his feet through the end of the peapod. He fell out onto the ground and stood up.

After a while, he started to feel strange. He bent down, and he drank some water from a small pool. The water ran down his throat, and he felt better.

When Man stood up, he saw a dark thing coming toward him. It stopped and looked at him.

This was Raven. Raven pushed his beak up onto his forehead like a mask and became a man.

The largest collection of totem poles in the world is in Ketchikan, Alaska. The carved wooden poles show characters from the ancient stories of the area's Native people.

"Where did you come from?" Raven asked. "I've never seen anything like you." He was surprised to see how much the man looked like himself.

"I came from that peapod," Man said, pointing at the vine with the broken pod still hanging on it.

"I made that vine!" Raven exclaimed. "But I didn't know anything like you would grow from it. Wait here."

He became a raven again and flew away. Four days later, Raven came back. He pushed his beak up and handed Man four berries.

"I made these for you," Raven said. "I want them to grow everywhere on Earth."

When Man had eaten the berries, Raven took him to a small creek. Man watched as Raven found some clay and formed a pair of tiny mountain sheep.

"Close your eyes," Raven said. He waved his wings four times over the clay figures, and they came to life as full-grown mountain sheep.

"Now look," Raven said to Man, pushing his beak up. Man was delighted with the sheep.

Raven made more animals. He made birds and fish. He made insects.

So that Man would not be lonely, Raven created a woman for him out of clay. Man loved Woman. More men were growing on the peapod vine. The world was filling up.

When a raven spreads its wings, they extend almost 4 feet (1.2 meters).

Dall sheep, which live in mountainous areas, are found in northwestern North America.

Raven watched Man and the other people. He saw how they took pleasure in all the things he made. But he started to worry that they would eat or destroy everything he had created.

Raven decided he should create something that would scare Man. He took some clay and shaped a bear, flapping his wings over it to make it come alive.

Bear stood up on his hind legs, and he shook himself. Then, he roared fiercely.

"Look," Raven said to Man, "I made this bear. He is very fierce, and if you disturb him, he will tear you to pieces."

Bears in Alaska stand as tall as 10 feet (3 m) on their hind legs.

Native people all over the northern parts of North America tell stories like that one. The Native Americans who live in Alaska tell many stories about Raven. They say that he created the world.

The stories are used to teach listeners and readers about respecting the world. In this story, Raven sees that Man can be dangerous. So, he creates Bear to keep Man from destroying things.

Native Americans have long respected nature and the land they live on. The Native peoples of ancient times did not think they owned land. They just lived on the land and used it. They taught their children that they were a part of Earth.

The Europeans who came to North America beginning in 1492 did not see the land in this way. They had different ideas. In Europe, there was not very much open land left. There were more people around. People who could afford it could pay to use land owned by lords or other powerful people. However, land ownership was not possible for most European people.

This is one reason so many Europeans were excited to go to the Americas. There was so much land for the taking. Nearly everyone could own land or at least work on the land.

In the 1600s, many people left England to claim land in North America. They included the group known as the Pilgrims, who landed in what is now Massachusetts.

Only one known cultural group, the Piraha of the Amazon Rainforest, has no creation story.

Up to **18 million Native people** lived in what is now the United States and Canada in **1492**.

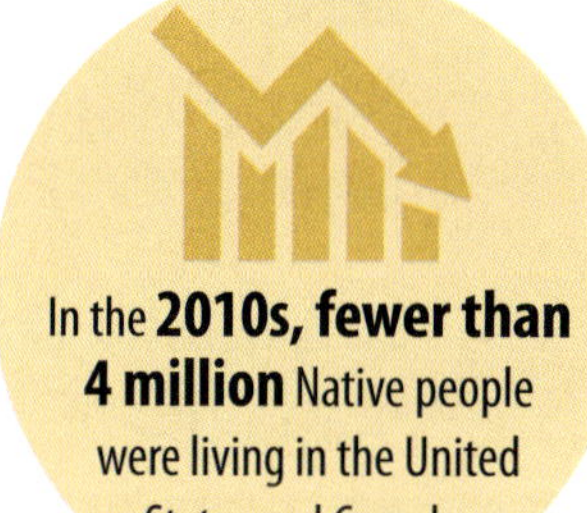

In the **2010s, fewer than 4 million** Native people were living in the United States and Canada.

Often, Europeans thought nature was something to fight. Many of them thought nature was cruel. Weather, as well as animals, could kill human beings. So, they believed that humans needed to overcome and change nature.

This was very different from what the Native Americans thought. They thought of themselves as being part of nature. They could not fight something of which they were a part.

Over time, Europeans started taking over more of North America. Many of the settlers did not care that Native Americans lived on the land first. By the 1800s, many white settlers believed that they had the right to spread out as far as they could. They thought they should take over all the land from the Atlantic to the Pacific Ocean. Many of them believed that God had given them that right. This idea was called "Manifest Destiny."

Not all the people felt that way, however. There were always some people who wanted to protect the most beautiful parts of the continent. They wanted to make sure that nature was not destroyed.

Wrangell-St. Elias National Park, in Alaska, is one of the areas the United States has set aside in order to protect its resources and features.

Eventually, more Americans realized that there were many important places in the United States that might be in danger. So, they asked the government to set aside these lands and protect them. No one could live on protected lands. Nobody could build stores there. People could visit these special areas, though.

Denali National Park, in Alaska, features the highest mountain in North America.

The United States set up a system of national parks. By 2018, a total of 59 national parks had been created. There were many more trails, seashores, and other areas set aside, as well.

The U.S. government protects hundreds of special areas where people can go to appreciate nature. However, Americans still do not always agree about how the natural riches found in these places should be used. For example, there are large parts of Alaska that people disagree about.

GET THINKING

In the Beginning

Almost every group of people has its own stories to explain how the world began. Often, these stories were first passed down from one person to another by word of mouth. Over time, many of the stories were finally written down. Have you learned creation stories from your family or others in your community? How are your stories different from the story about Raven? Are they the same in any way?

Chapter Two

The Story of Alaska

Alaska is very far north. It's not connected to any other part of the United States. However, Alaska does share a border with Canada. It is also very close to eastern Russia, which is on the continent of Asia. In fact, Russia is not many miles (kilometers) across the water from the Alaskan coast. The two places are separated by the Bering Sea.

Alaska is huge. The main part of the state is very large. In the south, the part of Alaska called the Aleutian Islands stretches 1,000 miles (1,600 km) into the ocean. Alaska has many big mountains, too. The tallest mountain in the United States, Denali, is there. Alaska also has **tundra** and forests. It has **glaciers** and rivers.

The first people to reach Alaska arrived a long time ago. Back then, the sea level was lower. There was actually solid land, like a bridge, between Asia and North America. It is likely that people from Asia walked over the land bridge. Later, the sea rose again. Water filled up the connection between the continents. They are separated today.

In images taken from space, it is clear that Alaska and the eastern part of Russia share the same region.

Some of the early people who crossed over the land bridge kept on walking. Over time, they spread over all of what is now Canada and the United States. Some went farther south, into Mexico, Central America, and South America.

Beluga whales do well in the cold ocean waters near Alaska because they have, below their skin, a thick layer of blubber, or fat, that keeps them warm.

Each group of early Alaskan people lived a little differently. The Inupiat lived near the Bering Sea. They lived in big communities and built houses out of wood, soil, and whalebone. They ate whales, seals, and **caribou**.

The Yup'ik lived in southern Alaska. They depended on seals, whales, and salmon for food. Meanwhile, the Aleuts moved to the Aleutian Islands. They lived in small villages. Their fishers moved around following the fish. They ate sea lions, whales, and fish.

The Athabascans lived inland. They were not near the ocean. They spent a lot of time near rivers, and they moved around following herds of caribou. They ate the caribou and fished for salmon in the rivers.

The Tlingit and thc Tsimshian lived on the southern coast. These Native American groups built wood houses. They fished and hunted seals, deer, moose, and mountain goats.

Alaskan caribou weigh as much as 700 pounds (320 kilograms).

In the early 1700s, the Russian **czar** wanted to know if Asia and North America were connected or if there was water between them. He also wanted to know more about eastern Russia, known as Siberia, and the region around it. The czar sent Vitus Bering, a sailor from Denmark. Bering and his crew sailed 5,000 miles (8,000 km) to Siberia. It was a dangerous journey.

In 1728, Bering discovered that Asia and North America were not connected. However, it turned out that, at one place, there is only 53 miles (85 km) between the two bodies of land. That small strip of water later became known as the Bering **Strait**.

After Bering's discoveries, other Russian ships sailed to the region. When the Russians came to Alaska, things changed for the Native people who already lived there. Russian explorers brought back furs from Alaska. Many Russians liked the furs. They wanted more. People realized that they could make money by hunting sea otters, seals, and other animals for their fur. Slowly, Russians and others started moving east.

A sea otter's dense fur has about 1 million hairs per square inch (6.5 square centimeters). This fur keeps the animal warm, even in very cold water.

In the 1770s, Spain sent its own explorers to Alaska. At that time, the Spanish controlled what is today California. They were worried about having the Russians to the north of them, in Alaska. Spain decided to send its own people northward to try to claim the land first, so the Russians could not have it all.

On Vitus Bering's second trip to Alaska, in 1741, his ship was wrecked in a storm. Bering and many of his crew lost their lives.

The Spanish explorers discovered that the British were also interested in Alaska. The British wanted to see if there was a way to travel by boat through northern North America from the Atlantic Ocean to the Pacific. British explorers also wanted to find things to sell, such as furs.

One of these British explorers was James Cook. On a voyage in 1778, he carried otter furs from western North America to China. The furs were really popular with the Chinese, which gave the British even more places where they could sell the furs they got from Alaska.

The Spanish, British, and Russians fought over the right to use the land in Alaska. Few of them really cared that there were already people living there. Meanwhile, the Native people did not want these strangers taking away their land and homes. Almost all of the explorers wanted furs, and they killed many animals. The Natives needed those animals for food and clothes. The Native people killed only the animals that they needed, but the Europeans killed everything they found. Often, they took only an animal's fur and wasted the rest of the animal.

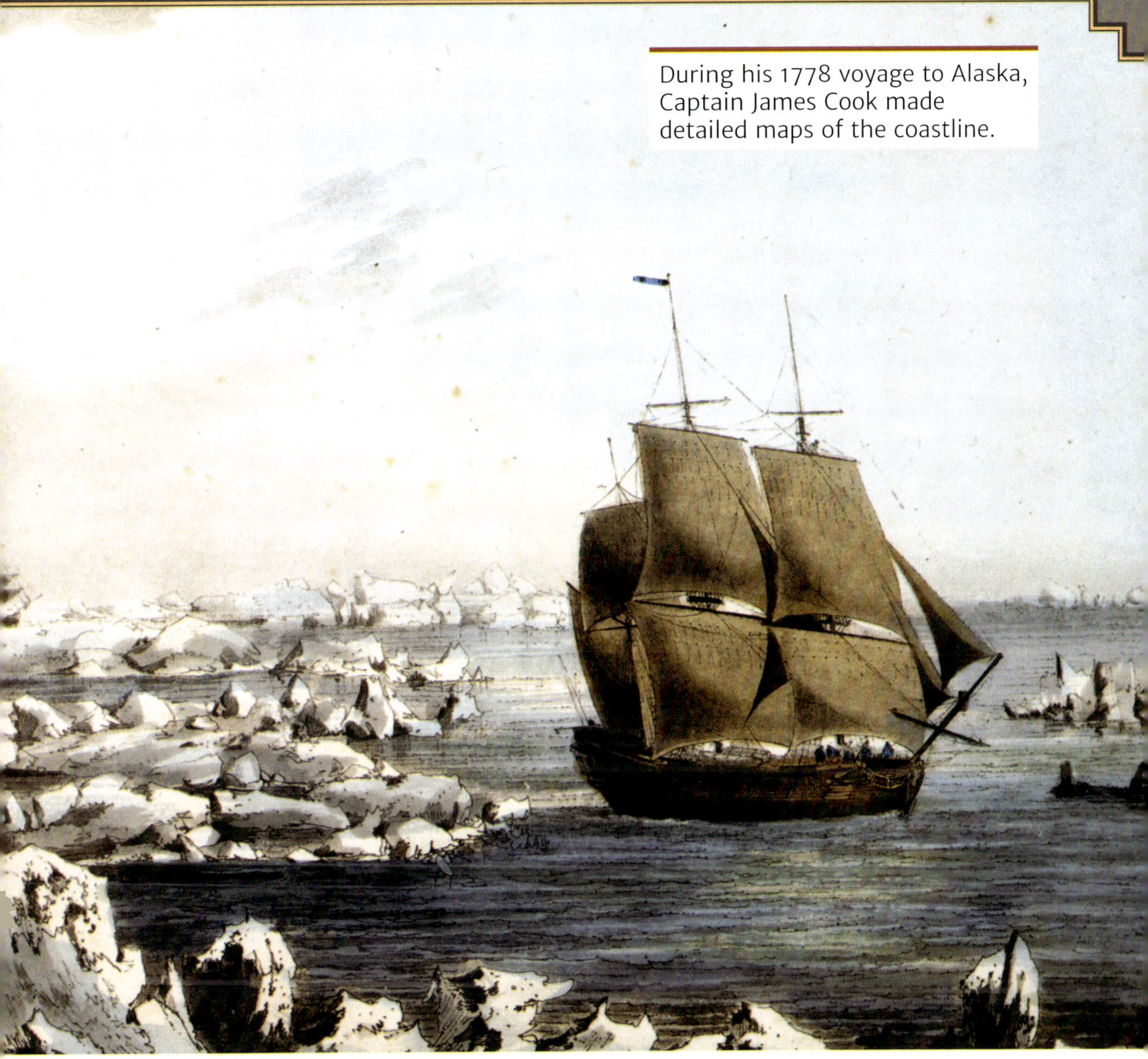

During his 1778 voyage to Alaska, Captain James Cook made detailed maps of the coastline.

The entire **coastline** of Alaska is **6,640 miles** (10,690 km) long.

Russians took **187,000 animal furs** from Alaska between 1743 and 1799.

Maps made by James Cook during his explorations were used by sailors for the next **200 years**.

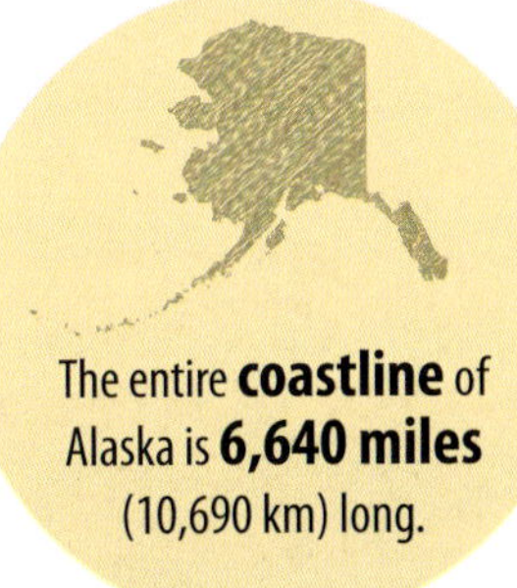

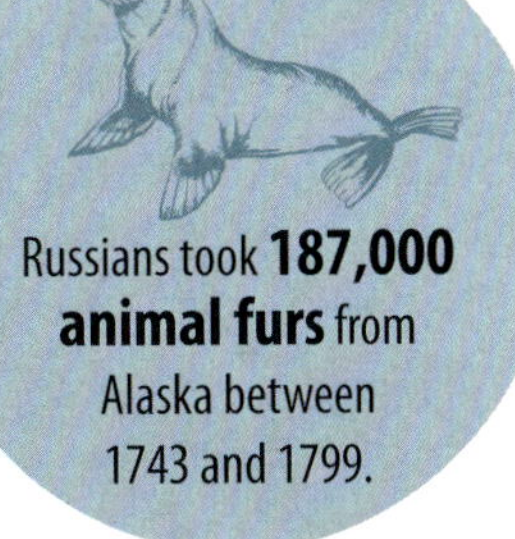

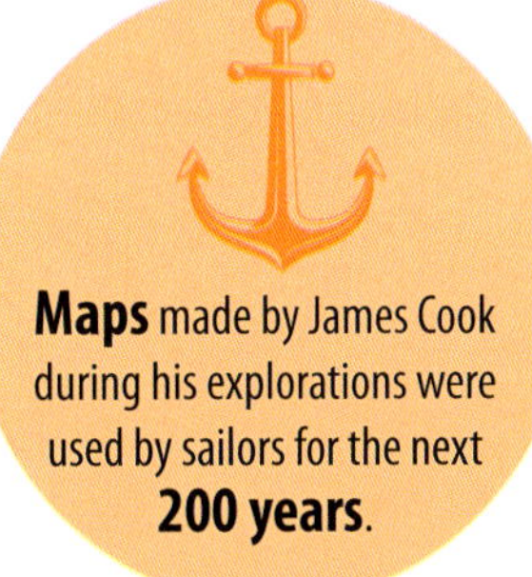

The Aleuts lived side-by-side with Russians and were the first Native group in North America to live with Europeans. However, the two groups did not really get along. The Aleuts protested the killing of the animals. Meanwhile, the Russians had better weapons. They often forced the Aleuts to work for them.

The Russians also brought diseases with them. The Aleuts had never run into the germs that caused these diseases. They were new germs that their bodies had never contacted. Their bodies could not fight off the germs the ways the Russians' bodies could. Many of the Aleuts died.

Russian trading companies tried to deal with the Native people peacefully. It was better for everyone when they could trade for things. However, the peace did not last. When a Russian company tried to set up a city, the company chose a place right in the middle of the area where the Tlingit lived. The Tlingit were not happy. They killed some of the Russians. Then, the Russians attacked the Tlingit.

In the end, the Russians decided to give up their American fur trade. Then, there was no more reason for them to hang on to Alaska. The Russians wanted to get rid of Alaska, but they did not want the British to get it. So, they sold the land to the United States.

The Russian-American Company was formed by the Russian government to make trading settlements in North America and to collect furs. The company used large ships to carry the furs to Russia.

THE RUSSIAN ORTHODOX CHURCH

Russia eventually left Alaska, but the Russian Orthodox Church did not. The Orthodox Church is the largest Christian faith in Russia. During the 1800s, Russians set up a church system in Alaska. One leader in this effort was Father Ivan Veniaminov. He grew up in Russia, but he wanted to be a priest in the Aleutian Islands. Many Aleuts liked him. He came to them in peace, and he learned their language. He gave the Aleuts more respect than most Russians did. Father Veniaminov even wrote books and a dictionary in the Aleuts' language. No one had ever written the language down before.

Some Aleuts became Christians because of Father Veniaminov. He could talk to them about his religion in Aleut. Many of them started attending his church services. Then, he went to the Tlingit, and they liked him, too. He offered to give the Native people shots against smallpox, which saved many lives. Eventually, he became a bishop in the Russian Orthodox Church. Then, he sent other priests to travel around Alaska and build churches. Some of those churches still exist today.

Chapter Three

Claiming Alaska

Compared to the land that makes up the other 48 U.S. states on the North American mainland, Alaska is a recent addition to the United States. At first, many people were unsure whether Alaska was worth its cost and trouble. However, Americans came to realize that the Alaskan land was well worth it.

One man, a lawyer and politician named William Seward, was in charge of buying the Alaskan land from Russia. In 1867, Seward signed a **treaty** with the Russians. As part of the agreement, the United States paid Russia $7 million.

The agreement that Russia made with the United States to hand over Alaska was signed on March 30, 1867.

When the Americans took over Alaska, there were still some Russians living there. They were given three years to move. The Russians were also offered the choice to stay and become U.S. **citizens**. However, the Native peoples who lived in Alaska were not offered United States citizenship at that time.

At first, most people did not think that Alaska would prove to be very useful. To many people, it was just a big place filled with snow and ice. However, Seward knew it was a wise purchase. Seward and others wanted the United States to keep growing. Buying Alaska made this possible.

Sitka, called New Archangel by its Russian settlers, was one of the largest towns in Alaska when the United States gained control of the region in 1867.

Bering Glacier in Alaska, which in recent years can be seen in images taken from space, is the largest glacier in North America.

In the beginning, the United States government declared Alaska an "Indian Territory" and sent the U.S. Army to build forts there. Few people knew what should or could be done with the area. For most of the 1800s, the United States did not even set up a government for the territory.

The United States paid Russia **2 cents per acre** (less than 1 cent per hectare) for Alaska.

Then, John Muir took his first trip to Alaska. Muir was a **naturalist**, scientist, and traveler. Before going to Alaska, he spent many years exploring and studying mountains in many parts of the American West. On October 25, 1879, he reached the Alexander **Archipelago**, off the coast of southern Alaska. It was cold and rainy, with a bitter wind. Despite the weather, Muir and the people he traveled with set out to see what were sometimes called the ice mountains, or glaciers.

At **26 miles** (42 km) long, **Matanuska Glacier** is the largest Alaskan glacier that can be reached by motor vehicle.

The Alexander Archipelago includes about **1,100 islands**.

At noon, they saw their first glacier. Muir looked up in awe at the mountain of ice towering above them. He was overcome with how much power the glacier had. This was nature at its most awesome.

Muir shared what he learned about Alaska. Many people who read about it were impressed. They started to travel to see the glaciers, mountains, and coasts there. It was clear that Alaska was a great place for tourists to see.

MUIR'S CLUB

John Muir was born in Scotland, but he was raised in the United States. He was a scientist who studied plants and ***geology****. He was also an inventor.*

When he was young, he was in an accident. He was blind for a little while. When he got his eyesight back, he decided to see as much of the world as he could. He walked around many parts of the United States. When he eventually made it to the Yosemite region, in California's Sierra Nevada mountains, he loved the place. Muir started writing about what he saw. He urged other people to travel and see the wonders he had seen.

Muir believed that people should protect the wondrous places of Earth. He could see that human beings were destroying some of the country's most beautiful land. So, he eventually started a group called the Sierra Club. The goal of the group was to protect valuable places in the United States. The Sierra Club still exists today.

Despite Muir's efforts, some people still grumbled about Alaska. The money spent to buy it seemed wasted to them. Many other people forgot that Alaska was even part of the United States. Then, gold was discovered in the region, and things changed.

In 1896, gold was found on the Klondike River in Canada. The site was very close to Alaska. The discovery started a gold rush. Soon, gold diggers flooded into the area. They looked in Alaska's rivers, hoping to find gold.

Miners also searched on Alaska's beaches. They looked up and down the Alaskan mountains. Thousands of people were digging for gold in many areas.

Some areas produced no gold. However, gold was discovered along the Alaskan coast, near the present-day city of Nome. Besides the miners, there were many people who moved to Alaska because of the Klondike gold rush. People started stores and other businesses. They sold the miners supplies and other things they needed.

All of a sudden, many more people were living in Alaska. From 1890 to 1900, the population doubled. There were 63,000 people by 1900.

The settlers built roads and towns. They also brought crime and disorder with them. The leaders of the United States began to realize that Alaska needed some sort of government now that more people were going to live there.

During the gold rush in Alaska, miners were known to dig just about anywhere, including the streets of their towns.

Alaska proved to have natural riches of many kinds. Even before the Klondike gold rush, some gold had been found in Alaska. People discovered that, besides gold, Alaska had plenty of fish, especially salmon. **Canneries** opened up in several areas.

Americans took as many fish as they wanted each spring, when the salmon showed up in large numbers. The towns with canneries would fill with workers. At the beginning there was plenty of fish for all. However, as years passed, there were not many fish left for the Native fishers. This, too, was a problem for the Native people.

FINDING OIL IN ALASKA

In 1968, oil was discovered in northern Alaska. The area had more oil than almost anywhere else in the United States. The country needed fuel for cars and factories. Fuel made from oil was important to America. However, the Alaska oil was found on land owned by Native people.

In 1971, the U.S. government passed a law that gave the Native people in Alaska $963 million in exchange for the land where the oil was located. The next step was to figure out how to get the oil out of Alaska. After all, Alaska lies far to the north of most of the United States.

The United States decided to build a pipeline, the Trans-Alaska Pipeline, to carry the oil to the nearest port. This port was about 800 miles (1,300 km) south of the area where oil was found. The pipeline would have to go through mountains and across bogs, or areas where the ground is soft and wet. It was finally completed in 1977. Today, a number of companies produce oil and use the Trans-Alaska Pipeline. They pay taxes to support people in Alaska.

In the early 1900s, railroads were built. The trains made it easier to get around Alaska and to send goods to other regions. The Alaskan land was also full of trees that could be used for lumber, which was shipped by train to the south.

To build Alaska's railroads, bridges were put up over many waterways.

The Klondike gold rush ended in 1912, and the number of people in Alaska decreased in the years that followed. However, the U.S. government discovered that Alaska was a good place for military bases during World War II. The United States fought in that war from 1941 to 1945. After the fighting ended, many workers and soldiers stayed. On January 3, 1959, Alaska became a U.S. state. More than 200,000 people lived in Alaska by that time.

GET THINKING

The Trans-Alaska Pipeline

The Trans-Alaska Pipeline has made Alaska richer and provided fuel for other parts of the United States. It also has gotten in the way of animals living on the land around the pipeline. Sometime, oil spills out of the pipeline. Animals have died. Land has been spoiled. People still do not agree about the Trans-Alaska Pipeline. Some people say Alaska and the United States are better off because of it. Other people say that it hurt nature and was a mistake. What do you think? Should providing fuel be more important than protecting animals and nature? Should saving natural areas sometimes be more important?

Alaska's Natural Riches

1 Eagle

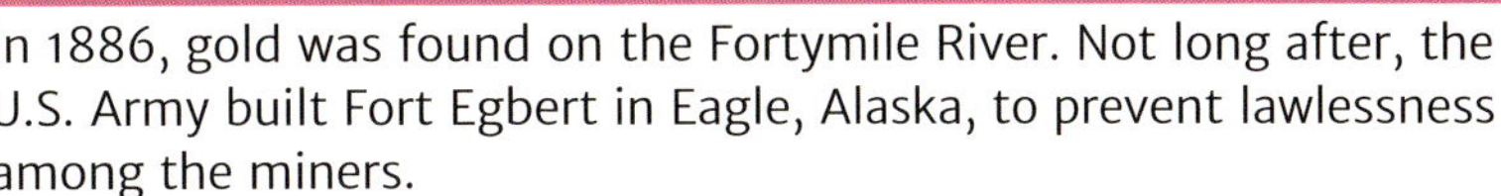

In 1886, gold was found on the Fortymile River. Not long after, the U.S. Army built Fort Egbert in Eagle, Alaska, to prevent lawlessness among the miners.

2 Ketchikan

By 1910, Ketchikan and other towns in southeastern Alaska had about two dozen sawmills, where tree trunks were cut into pieces of lumber. One-third of this lumber was used to make cases for canned salmon.

3 Skagway

Klondike Gold Rush National Historic Park, in Skagway, shows what life was like in gold rush towns. There are 20 buildings from the late 19th and early 20th centuries.

4 Prudhoe Bay

The 1968 discovery of oil was near Prudhoe Bay. This remote area in Alaska's far north has the coldest climate of any part of the state.

LEGEND

- Water
- City
- Capital
- Gold
-  Salmon
- Oil
- Highest Mountain
- Pipeline

Chapter Four

Protecting Nature

Throughout the 1800s, Americans spread across much of North America. They kept pushing west, and what they saw along the way amazed them. There were wide plains, huge mountains, and deep valleys. They saw huge trees and mighty rivers and ***geysers****.*

Many people wanted to protect the land and the natural features that they found. They did not want other people to ruin it all. So, they turned to the United States government and asked their representatives to set aside land that would be protected. Then, everyone could enjoy these spaces for a long time to come.

In the 1800s, Americans of European origin "discovered" what would later become Yosemite National Park. Native people had known about this area for a very long time. Among the first people of European origin to see Yosemite was a small group of men in the U.S. Army. The men were exploring a large area of California in 1851. Their job was to find Native Americans and force them to leave.

The men were stunned by the beauty that they saw. They called the place Yosemite. This was a name they had heard Native people call the Native Americans who lived there.

In 1861, a young photographer named Carleton Watkins visited Yosemite. He took pictures, which were put on display in New York City. Now, the rest of the country could see how amazing this place was. In response, more Americans traveled to Yosemite and found out how beautiful it is.

El Capitan, in Yosemite, is a giant rock and a popular place for rock climbers.

A senator from California came up with a plan to save Yosemite. He proposed a law that would protect the land. Nobody could build on it or live there. In 1864, President Abraham Lincoln signed the law. There were many other things going on then, such as the Civil War, but the president knew that this was important, too.

Other places in the West were getting attention, too. During this time, non-Native Americans also found Yellowstone. At first, no one believed the stories of the people who had seen it. There were geysers that shot up boiling water. There were steaming pools. Eventually, people were convinced. Scientists went to Yellowstone, and so did photographers.

Nearly a decade after the law to save Yosemite, President Ulysses S. Grant made Yellowstone a national park. It was the very first park to be run by the national government. It was also the first national park in the world. In the beginning, Yellowstone was basically owned by a railroad company. The man who was in charge of running Yellowstone also worked for the Northern Pacific Railroad. Taking a train on the Northern Pacific Railroad was one of the few ways that people could visit Yellowstone. The railroad made a great deal of money.

Yosemite was the next area to be declared a national park. The land at Yosemite was already protected. However, in 1890, it became an official national park.

Yellowstone National Park has more than 45 waterfalls. The tallest is the Lower Falls of Yellowstone Falls.

Yosemite National Park covers **1,200 square miles** (3,100 square kilometers).

Native Americans had lived in the Yosemite area for **4,000 years** before people of European origin arrived.

Carleton Watkins took **30 photographs** of Yosemite during his 1861 visit to the area.

Chapter Five

The National Parks

Today, there are 417 places associated with the United States National Park Service. That includes the 59 national parks. It's impossible to explore all of the parks from end to end. They are just too big. However, some people try to visit all of them.

National parks can be created by an act of Congress. The United States agreed to protect Yellowstone, the very first national park, in 1872. This became the basis for the rest of the national parks in the country.

Yellowstone is mostly in Wyoming. Parts of it stretch into Montana and Idaho. It has lakes, mountains, canyons, and rivers. It has a lot of **geothermal** features, such as hot springs. The most famous part of Yellowstone is Old Faithful Geyser. Old Faithful sends boiling water hundreds of feet (m) into the air.

The geyser is called Old Faithful because it erupts pretty regularly. It shoots water up about every 90 minutes. Sometimes, there is a little less time between eruptions, and sometimes, there is a little more. However, it always happens. Yellowstone has a wide variety of different animals as well. Grizzly bears, elk, mountain goats, wolves, and bison all live there.

The water in Old Faithful is 204 degrees Fahrenheit (96 degrees Celsius).

U.S. National Parks

California has nine national parks, the most of any state.
Alaska ranks second with eight national parks.

Carlsbad Caverns

Crater Lake

Grand Canyon

Park Name	State or Area	Year Created
Acadia	Maine	1919
American Samoa	American Samoa	1988
Arches	Utah	1971
Badlands	South Dakota	1978
Big Bend	Texas	1944
Biscayne	Florida	1980
Black Canyon of the Gunnison	Colorado	1999
Bryce Canyon	Utah	1928
Canyonlands	Utah	1964
Capitol Reef	Utah	1971
Carlsbad Caverns	New Mexico	1930
Channel Islands	California	1980
Congaree	South Carolina	2003
Crater Lake	Oregon	1902
Cuyahoga Valley	Ohio	2000
Death Valley	California, Nevada	1994
Denali	Alaska	1917
Dry Tortugas	Florida	1992
Everglades	Alaska	1947
Gates of the Arctic	Montana	1980
Glacier	Alaska	1910
Glacier Bay	Arizona	1980
Grand Canyon	Arizona	1919
Grand Teton	Wyoming	1929
Great Basin	Nevada	1986
Great Sand Dunes	Colorado	2004
Great Smoky Mountains	Wyoming	1929
Guadalupe Mountains	Nevada	1986
Haleakala	Hawai'i	1916

Park Name	State or Area	Year Created
Hawai'i Volcanoes	Hawai'i	1916
Hot Springs	Arkansas	1921
Isle Royale	Michigan	1940
Joshua Tree	California	1994
Katmai	Alaska	1980
Kenai Fjords	Alaska	1980
Kings Canyon	California	1940
Kobuk Valley	Alaska	1980
Lake Clark	Alaska	1980
Lassen Volcanic	California	1916
Mammoth Cave	Kentucky	1941
Mesa Verde	Colorado	1906
Mount Rainier	Washington	1899
North Cascades	Washington	1968
Olympic	Washington	1938
Petrified Forest	Arizona	1962
Pinnacles	California	2013
Redwood	California	1968
Rocky Mountain	Colorado	1915
Saguaro	Arizona	1994
Sequoia	California	1890
Shenandoah	Virginia	1935
Theodore Roosevelt	North Dakota	1978
Virgin Islands	U.S. Virgin Islands	1956
Voyageurs	Minnesota	1975
Wind Cave	South Dakota	1903
Wrangell-St. Elias	Alaska	1980
Yellowstone	Wyoming, Montana, Idaho	1872
Yosemite	California	1890
Zion	Utah	1919

Hawai'i Volcanoes

Shenandoah

Virgin Islands

Sequoia National Park has more than 8,000 giant sequoia trees.

Sequoia National Park was founded the same year as Yosemite, in 1890. It is located in California. This park is full of mountains. Sequoia has the highest point in the mainland United States south of Alaska. That point is the top of Mount Whitney.

The park's name comes from the giant sequoia trees that grow there. These trees are taller than most buildings. The largest tree on Earth grows in Sequoia National Park. It is called General Sherman. This tree stands 275 feet (84 m) tall.

Sequoia's trees are also very old. The oldest have been alive for more than 3,500 years. The people who set aside the area as a national park wanted to make sure that these trees survived. Many visitors still come to see them today. Each year, Sequoia National Park receives about 1 million visitors.

Snow that has melted in the Sierra Nevada mountains provides water for the Kaweah River, which runs through Sequoia National Park.

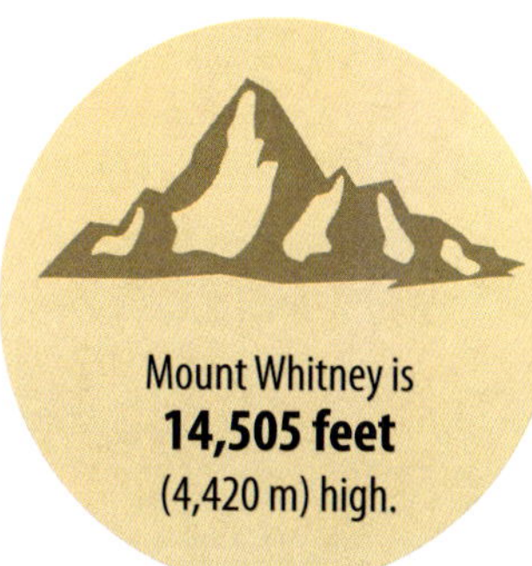

Mount Whitney is **14,505 feet** (4,420 m) high.

Sequoia National Park covers **629 square miles** (1,629 sq. km).

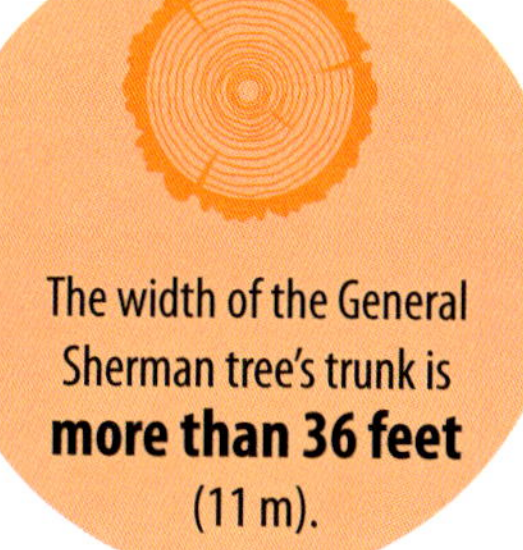

The width of the General Sherman tree's trunk is **more than 36 feet** (11 m).

Alpine azalea is a kind of flower that blooms in the tundra in Denali National Park.

The mountains in California's national parks were formed over millions of years by powerful forces deep within Earth. Those forces are still at work. In areas such as Yosemite, mountains are still very slowly becoming taller.

Many Americans wanted the government to protect places such as Yosemite. Besides its mountains, Yosemite National Park has forests, cliffs, streams, and sequoia trees. Many species, or types of living things, thrive there, where they can live mostly in peace. For example, the national park is home to bobcats, cougars, deer, owls, bats, and black bears.

The United States is a very big place. It has many cities and towns and a lot of farmland. However, the United States also has many areas filled with natural wonders. Having national parks helps the country's people hang on to vast areas of wilderness.

For example, the state of Alaska is filled with nature's riches. People can learn from Alaska and other beautiful places like it. Many Americans have come to the conclusion that these areas are needed and that people should take care of them, as the Native peoples did.

GET THINKING

Special Places on Earth

People protect large land areas for many reasons. The land is often protected because of its beauty. The area may also be set apart because of the variety of life found there. Research one of the U.S. national parks. Where is it? What are some of its special features? How and why was it chosen? Do you think the decision to protect the area was right? Why?

Yosemite's mountains grow about 1 foot (0.3 m) taller every 1,000 years.

Timeline

28,000–13,000 BC—Native peoples travel to North America across a land bridge that then connected Russia to Alaska.

1728—Bering travels on the rough waters of what is now called the Bering Sea.

1834—Father Ivan Veniaminov of the Russian Orthodox Church arrives in Alaska.

13,000 BC | **1725** | **1800** | **1850**

1851—A group of U.S. soldiers travels through the Yosemite region.

1725—Czar Peter the Great of Russia sends Vitus Bering to discover whether Russia is connected to North America.

1864—President Abraham Lincoln signs the Yosemite Grant Act, a law intended to preserve Yosemite.

1896—After gold is found in Canada's Yukon Territory, many people arrive in nearby Alaska to search for the valuable metal.

1865 | 1875 | 1885 | 1895

1867—The United States buys Alaska from Russia.

1872—President Ulysses S. Grant makes Yellowstone the first national park.

1890—Sequoia becomes a national park in September, followed by Yosemite in October.

Quiz

ONE
About how many Native people were living in what is now the United States and Canada in 1492?

TWO
How many national parks did the United States have as of 2018?

THREE
What is the name of the thin strip of water that separates Russia and Alaska?

FOUR
Which Native group lived on Alaska's southern coast long ago, besides the Tlingit?

FIVE
In which year did John Muir make his first trip to Alaska?

SIX
Who started the Sierra Club?

SEVEN
In which year was oil discovered in Alaska?

EIGHT
What was the first U.S. national park?

NINE
Today, how many places are associated with the U.S. National Park Service?

TEN
Which national park has the highest point in the mainland United States south of Alaska?

ANSWERS

ONE up to 18 million TWO 59 THREE the Bering Strait
FOUR the Tsimshian FIVE 1879 SIX John Muir
SEVEN 1968 EIGHT Yellowstone
NINE 417 TEN Sequoia

Key Words

archipelago: a group of islands

canneries: factories where food is processed into ready-to-eat products and put into cans

caribou: large reindeer that live in northern North America

citizens: people who have full legal rights in the country where they live

czar: a Russian ruler, similar to a king

geology: the study of Earth and its history

geothermal: related to heat that comes from inside Earth

geysers: springs that send shoots of hot water into the air

glaciers: large masses of ice that are very slowly moving

naturalist: someone who studies nature

strait: a narrow strip of water, with land on both sides, that connects two larger bodies of water

treaty: a written agreement between two or more countries

tundra: frozen land without trees or bushes, found in Earth's far-northern regions

Index

LIGHTBOX

SUPPLEMENTARY RESOURCES

Click on the plus icon found in the bottom left corner of each spread to open additional teacher resources.

- Download and print the book's quizzes and activities
- Access curriculum correlations
- Explore additional web applications that enhance the Lightbox experience

LIGHTBOX DIGITAL TITLES
Packed full of integrated media

VIDEOS

INTERACTIVE MAPS

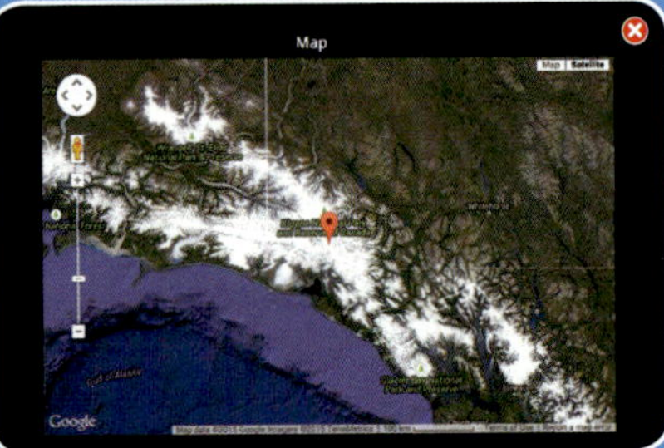

WEBLINKS

SLIDESHOWS

QUIZZES

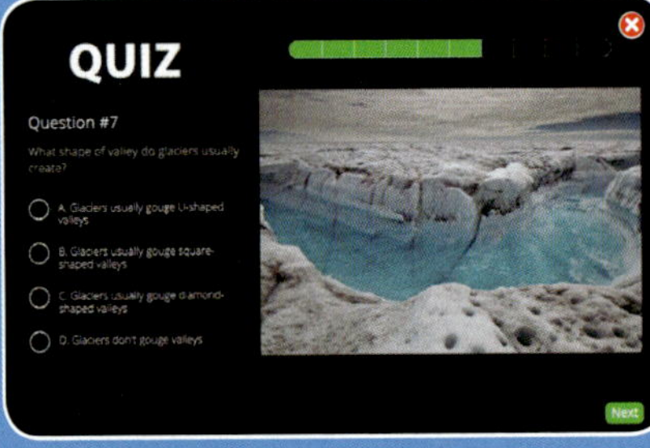

OPTIMIZED FOR

- ✓ TABLETS
- ✓ WHITEBOARDS
- ✓ COMPUTERS
- ✓ AND MUCH MORE!

Published by Smartbook Media Inc.
350 5th Avenue, 59th Floor
New York, NY 10118
Website: www.openlightbox.com

First published by Mason Crest in 2013

062018
121117

Library of Congress Cataloging-in-Publication Data
Names: Windsor, Wesley, author.
Title: American Wilderness, 1865-1890 / Wesley Windsor.
Description: New York, NY : Smartbook Media Inc., 2019. | Series: How America Became America | Includes index. | Identifiers: LCCN 2017054968 (print) | LCCN 2018003934 (ebook) | ISBN 9781510536050 (Multi User ebook) | ISBN 9781510536043 (hardcover : alk. paper)
Subjects: LCSH: Alaska--History--Juvenile literature. | National parks and reserves--United States--History--Juvenile literature.
Classification: LCC F904.3 (ebook) | LCC F904.3 .W55 2019 (print) | DDC 979.8--dc23
LC record available at https://lccn.loc.gov/2017054968

Printed in Brainerd, Minnesota, United States
1 2 3 4 5 6 7 8 9 0 22 21 20 19 18

Project Coordinator Heather Kissock
Art Director Terry Paulhus

Photo Credits
Every reasonable effort has been made to trace ownership and to obtain permission to reprint copyright material. The publisher would be pleased to have any errors or omissions brought to its attention so that they may be corrected in subsequent printings.

The publisher acknowledges Getty Images, Alamy, Newscom, Shutterstock, and iStock as its primary image suppliers for this title.